VICTORY FOR
THE SLAIN

WALMER POETRY

The Pelican Island by James Montgomery
Poems by Katherine Mansfield
Victory for the Slain by Hugh Lofting

VICTORY FOR THE SLAIN

by

Hugh Lofting

SANDNESS
MICHAEL WALMER
2020

Victory for the Slain first published 1942

This edition published 2020

by

Michael Walmer
North House
Melby
Sandness
Shetland ZE2 9PL

ISBN 978-0-6486909-4-8 hardcover

To

my brother

ERIC

I

SWINGING in step,

In sweat, they pass me,

These khakied squads of infantry,

As, more old and slow, from Town

I climb Northminster Hill.

Queer, how the beat of military drill

Can wrench my nerves and brain so tight

With that infernal, '*Left!* . . . . .

'*Left, right!* . . . . *Left, right!*'

Perhaps my very thinking's out of step.

They fade. And soon,

Long shadows stretching into afternoon,

I come upon a soldier all alone,

Here seated on the High Street's curb of stone.

The blue of hospital he wears.

His fingers fumble matches on his knee.

Perplexed I wonder — then I see

How awkwardly he tries to get

A flame up to his cigarette

With one remaining hand — his *left*.

Far off and faint: '*Left!* . . . . .

  '*Left, right!* . . . . *Left!* . . . . .

  Relaxed, he puffs

And smiles in thankfulness because

To help him he had seen me pause.

  Lest we forget!

Around his feet lie matches' embers.

If we forget he still remembers.

His features pale show no regret;

But with his mates — and thousands yet,

  Can he forget?

Lest tears he'll see,

I turn — continue up the hill;

But as I go my old eyes fill;

And helplessly

My mind recalls the dirge refrain:

In war the only victors are the slain.

Sergeants for recruitment

And again the fluttering girls!

So much for philosophy's analysis

Versus the immediacy of present need.

At day's end, like a weary peasant

Returning to the peace of home,

To refuge from the Now and Present,

Of evenings,

To this edifice I come.

As I approach

The summit of the hill,

It slowly dawns

From curved horizon into view

    And zenithward ascends from earth anew.

    Grey, silhouetted belfry,

How your circling rooks still cry

And glide against that glowing, twilit sky

Whose roseate dusks of promise calmed,

Or blood-red dawns of storm alarmed

    The shepherds through millennia!

    Set back

Where meaner buildings may not spoil

The vista to those centuries of toil,

This song, this melody in stone,

Here chanted by the generations gone,

Now beckons my wearying feet toward

Its verdant, wide and welcoming sward.

   'Come unto me!'

  Three gentle flights of steps converge
To platform, where the triptych doors
Their greys of oak with greys of limestone merge;
And, glorious, the façade soars
Up where, now sun-tipped, greys of stone
With lavenders of clouds, in tone,
Blend pallid finials with the sky;
And Man's enraptured works to God's reply
  Translucent tints of dreaming harmony.

  What if their *planes* come over this
  With unseeing eyes of Science!

  How strange,
That even as my fingers grasp
The ancient portal's eaten hasp
The blatant noises of To-day

In murmurs mould and melt away:

The railway train, the car's harsh horn,

Mellowed into Past, reborn,

   Now change to bygone, more melodious

                                    strains.

   Silent on its hinges,

The massive oak swings to.

The weighty latch drops softly

With its dull metallic click

And no reverberating echo's rumble

   Betrays my entrance here.

   Within

In humble solitude I stand,

Drinking the silence eloquently grand,

To lighten melancholy and to quench my pain.

My son, my dear, dead, happy son,

Like you,

   In war the only victors are the slain.

   My stature soon, inexplicably grown,

New-come from open air, alone,

Expands with lifting gratitude to face

The somehow greater greatness

   Of this walled-in space.

   Cruciform beatitude in stone!

Trinity in channels: nave

With aisle to left and aisle to right —

Sign of Western Cross, from left to right.

'*Left! . . . . Left, right!*' . . . . .

That thrice-accursed beat

   Still pounds within my brain.

   Proud architects of Past,

Princes in stateliness' design,

What paradox in grandeur and obscurity!

Your genius' modesty here shames

Our modern Art so publicized.

Call me the score:

How many who come here will know your

names?

For selves

You weighed as nought world-wide acclaims —

Anonymous identity and fate —

Content to let your hymns in stone relate

The praise of Craft.

In this you show, dead architects,

How truly you were great.

Walls,

Dear, treasuring walls

I hear you whispering your history

To hardened ears, your millennium of memories:

Sad requiem sung;

These banners and standards, tattered, hung;

The trophies of battle on alien soil,

Sole prizes of courage and suffering toil.

For these

How many in their graves are lain?

In war the only victors are the slain.

But, nave, you sing!

Vast nave, you still can sing!

Asperges twixt your flanking aisles;

Your columns of columns march unending —

Processioned stone,

Phalanxed and symmetric, wending,

Adeste! — Sing!

While candle-flames in worn, shined sconces

So gently sway their timed responses.

Here Nobodies with Somebodies, abreast,

In Faith paid homage with the rest.

Democracy immortal was defined

When majesty and poverty combined.

Sinners, saints and soldiers

Like these pillars of stone in line,

All levelled in the eyes of God,

To Future of the Futures, on they trod —

Eternity in front and Neverness behind.

Walls, we hear them sing.

High, vaulted roof your echoes find

And ring!

Sing, Acolytes equal,

Pauper and King!

There! — Was that a flash

I saw through incense-mist?

A gleam! — A naked sword?

Lord Abbot, *there*, my lord —

I beg you interfere —

If you would brook no brawling here.

Mad riots in cathedrals have been known

When wild Plantagenets have held the throne.

Was not staunch Becket slaughtered at the Mass

By Henry's barons?

It *is* a sword!

Forbid them, Abbot, this I pray —

Oh! . . . . God's mercy! . . . . Oh! . . . . .

   What are these words I say?

   Lord Abbot, your pardon!

My eyes and mind play tricks —

The incense —

I am ageing, Father — Let me sit. . . . .

Forgive my shortened breath —

   A murder, sacrilege, I feared.

   I wonder if the sacristan has heard —

Venerable guardian of the sanctuary-lamps,

The lamps that never quench —

What may he think, if at this bench,

Seeking voices strange and noises queer

He finds

This babbling nonentity a'nodding here? . . . . .

Abbot — or Sacristan — I meant . . . . Oh,

                                        breath!

    I meant no harm.

II

HOLY Water stoop; Poor Box.

Poor Box, receptacle for needy's aid,

What generations here their tribute made! —

Where all their sympathy might offer

   To your savings, humble little coffer.

I know your prayerful, lilting lullaby by heart:

None but the miserly ever forgot

Alms to let fall through this worn, fretted slot;

Ducats and guilders and guineas of gold,

Groats, silver crowns and the pennies untold,

Coinage from all the four quarters of Earth —

Pittance from pious in wealth or in dearth.

Poor, Poor Box!

I wish your open mouth could speak.

Were you, symbol of sweet Charity,

Sometimes abused? —

Philanthropy with ostentatious patronage

confused?

Money!

What has money, in its essence

Or as instrument of power, consigned us?

To hoard is not to earn —

Money-power in Past, as now,

Made continents in devastation burn.

And I, myself,

Have seen an antique watch of gold

Lying in an offertory-plate,

Dropped there by a widow

Who had nothing else to give.

But, Poor Box,

Your patient duty here was surely good:

To bring the destitute some help and food.

    Yes, give us the conservation of the earth,

The farm and food —

What futility to brood

    On pictures of the Past!

    And yet? . . . . Not yet so fast!

For Past can speak and Future call.

It is the Present,

Always you, accursed Present, stand accused

And your backsliding failure to foresee —

Forever blaming Circumstance,

The errors of your fathers and the exigence of

                        Chance

    To salve your careless conscience.

Deny that it was you! —

This unforeseeing you,

Who forged the flaws and faults

Into those fault-filled chains

You left for poor Posterity to drag

    Unlinking and unriddling along the years!

Ah, move on, so fatuous oracle! —

With your glib facility's

Cascading cataracts of glittering words —

Vainly bent to pack the wisdom of the ages

Plus Infinity's circling and perpetual motion

    Into a stanza bound and stopped!

Planes? . . . . The walls are strong.

The roof is frail . . . . They must not come!

From Poor Box

And from those who want

  To richly carved Baptismal Font.

  And there, nearby,

The bell-ropes, swayless, grouped,

From high and dim, pierced ceiling's dizzy fall,

Dreaming in potential pendance, hanging —

Clarion signallers for duty, for alarm or rest —

Composed, await the summoning clanging

Of Angelus hours' revolving call.

  Salve, Regina! . . . . .

  Inherited miseducation;

Long-cultured prejudice;

Propaganda's maledicted misdirection,

Made worse and wider now

By Modern Money's swifter sowing of untruth . .

Ave, Maria! . . . . .

Oh, unthinking little wisdom of our time,

There is no war, not bred of wars,

That was not nursed on lies!

Salve, Regina Angelorum! . . . . .

Motionless, bare-headed reapers praying,

Closed eyelids, and their forelocks straying —

Labour suaged by breath of gentle wind —

Simplicity's lilies in the field.

None but the criminal can be made

To plunge into a heart he was not taught to hate

A bayonet's cold unthinking blade.

Angelus Domini. . . . . .

Is it not equally to blame

To teach God's children, 'My Country, right or

wrong;'

'The White Man's Burden' — or that 'Right is

Might' —

Or that to dominion by conquest

For evermore they should proclaim

The dedication of their very race's name? . . . .

And the Angel of the Lord declared unto Mary. .

III

MY FOOTSTEPS rouse no sound

Or echo from the stone

As up the aisle I pass,

Walking on the epitaphs of Saxon abbots —

Great prelates whose dying lips requested

This ultimate humility in death:

That their remains be placed beneath a

                         pavement

Where feet of laity would tread

In coming to the Mass. . . . .

  'Aethelstan' and 'Elred!' . . . .

Wholesome, friendly Death,

You are no grim or morbid Reaper here.

Give me your hand again, as once you did

In Flanders, such a little time ago,

Some score of years and five.

  Neither Dunstan's sturdy heart

Nor this less valorous one of mine

Could suffer shock or hurt

From rubbing elbows with you,

Familiar neighbour Death; for here

  Life itself is but your twin in Hope.

  Dusk creeping on —

God grant those bombers of the air

  Hold off a while at least!

  Little door;

Little door, half-open.....

Open? — No one robs a church —

Not openly.

  King John — or Henry Tudor? . . . . .

Beyond, I see a strip of well-clipped grass

Where plump blue pigeons strut,

Searching and pecking in the sod —

    Friends of Saint Francis.

    Brave guardian cock!

Always on the watch — even at your feeding,

With your ruffled neck and scarlet eye

Tilting and craning now and then

To watch the sky

For hovering hawks.

    I've seen your instinct do the same

When silver of an aeroplane

Has flashed against the sunlit blue.

    The breeze so softly roughs

Blue feathers on your neck.

    Those planes! . . . . .

    Keep watching, keep watching, little cock!

What peace! — Such peace is here!

  Behind,

This sad side-altar where

Madonna of the Dolours grieves —

Dolores — symbol of World Sorrowing

                            enshrined —

To sacristy, I see a passage wind.

  Though windowless, this tunnel plain and bare

Shows serviceable walling, smoothly shined

  By brushing of a million surplice sleeves.

  Armorial sepulchres, embrasured tombs —

Prince-bishops, legates and great cardinals,

Seigneurs, hidalgos, margraves, earls,

Saxons, Norsemen, Normans, Celts —

Men of power, nobility of all the earth,

Goodly little league of nations

Now more closely and so ultimately leagued

   In death and peace!

   Cousins, some, to stout du Guesclin,

Captain whose brave heart fear never knew,

Whose widely famed escutcheon bore no stain —

Romance living by the sword

   And by its bright blade slain.

   Du Guesclin, fortitude's example!

Bear up, Free French,

Come lift your cross again —

The Cross of Survival, Cross of Salvation,

   The Cross of Crusade and Cross of Lorraine!

And see! — On coffin's lid of stone

Effigy of Chatelaine lying;

Little spaniel graven at her feet —

Sweet smile, Death's voicelessness defying —

Serenity lonely but complete.

No mate on twin sarcophagus emplaced!

Re-union with her love deferred? . . . . .

I read the epitaph almost defaced:

Her Knight's in Palestine interred.

His shield here, dented —

And a helmet gashed. . . . .

I see him now. . . . Look, look, the path he

slashed

To the rescue of the King!

On thundering horse with flying mane

He sunders the Saracen ranks apart

This friend of Richard the Lionheart.

'Plantagenet's down!' — Now risen again. . . . .

Victory? — Yes. But among the slain

Lies there your Knight! . . . . .

And they brought you back

   A shield!

   Hail to the Dead!

Hail, heraldry and pride of race,

Hail, lineage, emblazoned resting-place!

All hail to you,

   The equal and the peaceful Dead!

   May that be why you smile, sweet Chatelaine,

When this, a shield, War made your only gain?

No, no bitterness is here.

   How then may I account

This sunlight in your face,

Benevolence, this strength, this kindly grace,

   Triumphant, tranquil — as are the victors

                    slain?

Perhaps in life you too were fain

To warn a chivalry so brave but vain.

   Smile and sleep, dead Chatelaine!

Reward more worthy now is yours.

Our Day's too young to count the scores.

   In past you lived: for Future yearned.

Your lesson still we have not learned.

This peace, for which in life you sought,

To us, in after-life, you taught.

Dear, widowed but rewarded saint,

   Smile on!

IV

CHANCEL, enframed

Within the apexed arch

That leaps and springs

From Aspiration's humble feet to God!

　Like Crusade, where Cross and Crescent

Opposed — no medial — in Holy Land,

Here, ignoring querulous Present,

　Is Past to Future, bridging, spanned.

　So Memory to Hope is wedded

In nuptials of Man's dreams ideal;

And heirs of Motherhood so bedded

　May make his god-ambitions real.

　Yet, Deity of any Faith,

For Whom, the long millennium equal

To a tick upon our clock must be,

May we ephemera expect a sequel

From forebears of Eternity

Before Earth merges to another star?

   If here we boast of what we are,

Explain, All Knowing, what we were!

     And tell, Omnipotence, what we'll be!

     Ah, walls, maternal walls!

You must have wept your welcomes

When you saw

     Your coffined sons borne home from foreign

                                  war!

     My mourning walls,

Brave bastions of bygone years,

Can these wet bead-drops be your tears

For Knighthood in these tombs here sleeping,

So still in death, dead vigil keeping?

Or are they testaments of sorrow

For Yesterday, To-day, To-morrow —

For stubborn man's refusal to disbar

　The futile frenzy of recurrent War?

　Walls, these statued figures wait

Beneath your sheltering arms

Like spectres dimmed

By gloom of coming nightfall,

As if despising all alarms

　Of iconoclast invaders. . . . .

　Magdalen to right; Saint Veronica to left;

High altar to the East; baptismal font to West;

Transept to the right; transept to the left;

Left, right! . . . . Left!

　What's this? — Is my mind bereft,

Possessed? — No!

I'm no madder than this world.

   This world has mind-plague —

And in quarter-centuries the fits return

And cause

With their accursed wars

   All building of the centuries to burn.

   I'm *not* mad!

And no one saw me enter.

If they should hunt me here

I'll escape and crash

The thunder-knocker on the giant door

   And cry,

'Abbot, Lord Abbot, let me in,

'Sanctuary! — Sanctuary I win

   While my fingers grasp the bronze!'

Left, right! — Left, right! . . . . Left!

What is this sticking in my brain,

Which stops the very blood

Of reason's flow?

    No!

Are they come again?

Most surely these are new!

Are not

The intervening years too few?

    It's every score of years and five

That they return —

Not now!

    Are these alive

Or spectres of the past, all slain?

    In War the only ones that yet lived on

Are gone —

The conquering slain.

    It is not time! . . . . *Halt!*

Left, right! . . . . Gauche, droit!

Links, rechts! . . . . Left, right! . . . .

       BATTALION. . . . Halt!

  Halt, oh, halt them, God of Hosts!

My sight's too weak to tell the ghosts

From men of flesh.

  And there's that flash again

Bayonet or broadsword? — Are not the twain

Fused here as one?

  They fade! . . . . They're gone!

  Sweet evening light!

Like my poor sight

So nearly blind,

You're dimming; but my mind

More clearly sees.

  Firm walls, bear up my faltering knees.

Give breath, give breath, dear breathing walls!

This soft light, too,

Upon your smooth strength falls.

   Tell me they'll not come again

With sacrilegious arms to stain

You, dear stronghold of sanity's regain!

   My reverent palms upon you press.

Accept my throbbing heart's caress

So thankful for the coolness of your stone;

And steady me this little space of time.

Burnt dry,

My lips brush moisture from your flaking lime.

   In you embraced,

No longer shall I fear to be alone,

My Sanctuary,

   My Sanctuary in stone!

V

MAN, God's poorest handiwork!

We, the *great!*

How much more great the tiny motes of dust

Dancing in these slanting beams

From tracery's glass

   Of amber, violet and rose!

   Yet, some of us were great —

It must be so.

   Perhaps, Omnipotence, long, long ago

You touched our hearts

With exaltation's lifting glow,

To kindle growth we never guessed —

To pull us through Dark Ages' guilt —

And thus this psalm in stone we built;

   But later slowly changed,

Unknowing that we cast away

Our tranquil stature day by day;

Till back to littleness we crept,

   Where, in oblivion, our visions slept.

And now,

We look at *this* and wonder how

   From hands like ours it ever came.

   Vain, vaunting Moderns,

In hectic, hurrying Science to despise

A way of life

   Whose gracious leisure was its dearest prize!

   A way of life: *Via Crucis!*

The Stations of the Cross unfold

The Calvary-pilgrimage around you, walls —

Recounting walls, who also tell

The trials which ancient chivalry befell,

Those sagas great and lessons grim

    That followed Resurrection's Hymn.

    That beat —

The tramp of marching feet? —

The whirr of starting planes at dusk or dawn!

Why must I mingle and confuse

These sounds and thoughts that muse

    So madly through my mind?

    Wars to end wars? — War again!

Must Mankind forever kill and kill,

Thwarting every decent dictate

    Of the human will?

War again! —

When well we know

    War's final victors always were the slain.

This apathy!

Our apathy in peace-time:

  The gallant ardour of this Youth for war!

  Poor, listless soldier, maimed,

Bravely trying to re-design

A shattered life

  With but a single hand!

  The little door sways, silent, in the breeze

As if, like my poor mind, it were in doubt

To yield or fight,

Swayed by force of World's wild winds —

Blowing left or right —

Now pulling from within

  Now pressed on from without.

When nation against nation

Shall at last lay down their arms,

Will Class against another come —

The Reds against the Whites?

  And faiths and races, too,

The Whites against the Blacks —

Mahommedan, the Christian, the Arab, and the

                                        Jew —

Must we admit this *We* against the *You*

  Forever shall return for solving?

  Will both these Armageddons seem

As naught but mere rebukes

For peace-time apathy of Past

When measured

With that more terrifying Social Storm,

The Second Flood, that broods

And quivers on the lintel of the door —

The little door half-open,

Providing closed-in Man

    His single entrance and his one escape?

    And still the statues wait

In serried, marble confidence

Trusting our humanity;

While flickers of a sanctuary lamp

Make deepening shadows rise and fall

    Behind their backs.

    Destroyers and oppressors all!

Attila and Tamerlane!

Savage Hun or Mongol horde!

Those stolen lands will not remain

In restful amity's accord,

    Or 'peace' dictated by a sword!

Dark memories of the Dead are long.

No 'order' can atone for Wrong.

Your children's children will disown

Your means — for which they can't atone

To justify dominion's end —

    And legacies they can't defend.

VI

GREAT Restfulness,
Dear, grateful restfulness!
Pagan and Papal, the romance,
  The story of this Rome!

The triple crown, the mitred majesty
And humility majestic;
The jewelled chalices, the altar-cloth of gold,
Imperial purple come to Easter Mass —
All stemming from the lowly cow-shed
Nigh to Bethlehem. . . . The East and West,
  Herod and Tiberius. . . . . .

Raiders!
Raiders from the sea, the land —
  Raiders from the air!

Great Papal Rome,

Who would not forswear

A second sacking of your Hallowed Home

By air?

You, past arbiter of Kings

And kingly conduct,

Mistakes of policy you may have made,

But never did you lend your sanction

To oppression of the lowly

Or destruction of the weak

By stronger realms.

And if now

A puffed-up, paltry Caesar hides behind

Your sacred vestments, Christian Rome,

Surely we can find

Other means to thwart his crumbling schemes

Than a Slaughter of the Innocents

    Or a razing of your treasury of Past.

    Let 'V' of Victory be ours;

But, with you, we never need invoke a 'V'

For *VENGEANCE Shall be Mine,*

Nor court the stigma of the 'V'

    For Vandals.

VII

LADY-CHAPEL, priedieu set for prayer,
Madonna sculptured from the marble of Carara,
With the Blessed Babe,
  Above the little altar wide enough for Mass.

  There, down below,
The reliquary — glass-fronted;
And within
Its treasuring, half-lighted, tiny vault
I glimpse the relics:
A bishop's ring; a blood-stained thorn;
Two finger-bones of some dead saint-evangelist
Who blessed the heathen on a distant shore
Long, long ago — the hand of Faith;
Knotted cords; some tinsel from a wreath
  And a rosary's broken beads.

Reliquaries under altars

And reliquaries under hearts — our own

Dim, mile-stoned memoranda:

Petals faintly fragrant

And the ferns pressed flat in prayer-books;

Memories of sparrows in a flowering garden

Near a cloister.

The priedieu's old and smooth and worn,

Some choir-boy's pocket-knife has cut

The letter 'M' into the oak. . . . .

Rosaries and litanies.

Loretto, loveliest of all the litanies —

Litany in stone!

Madonna, who would dare add words

To Loretto's masterpiece in literature of

prayer?

'Mirror of Justice, *Pray for us!*

'Tower of David, Seat of Wisdom,

'Spiritual Vessel, Health of the Sick,

'Queen of Angeles, Gate of Heaven,

'Morning Star, Tower of Ivory,

  'Mystical Rose, *Pray for us!*'

Who dares add words?

  But is there impiety

If we devise, Madonna,

Our own less lovely modern prayers? —

For of these, sinners have more need

  Than saints inspired.

  Dear, constant Sanctuary Light

Of Charity's Eternal Flame!

Fair Emblem-flower upon the shield! —

The shield brought back from bitterness

Of foreign war —

Maternal Symbol

Of all the great and good in human hearts!

Hold staunch and fast

This only shield for us, the shield of Peace

   That shall not pass away.

   And if eternal vigilance

Shall be the price,

Remind us of this vigil of the Dead,

The conquering slain, who here

So patient, silent, watch and wait;

And let us, that little price

Forever, as our debt of honour unto them

   Be grateful, ready and most glad to pay.

   Ave, Maria! — Ave, atque vale!

I can no longer kneel.

   My knees are stiff with age.

Your blessing, please, upon my shoulders

As I go.

Again my footsteps make no sound.

How did these architects of Past

Achieve this pin-drop quiet, so echoless,

Within their churches? —

Perhaps reaching for the hush of human longing

Through devotional repose.

And yet . . . . there is some sound.

The organ-loft? . . . . .

No, beyond the little door — outside.

I cannot see the grass; the light is dimmer.

Thunder. . . . *Tenebrae?* — Golgotha's Dark! . . . .

No, it's not the season for the service.

Listen! . . . . A drone!

That's it . . . . But is it in my ears alone?

A drone! That's it: a droning in the sky! . . . . .

A drone of aeroplanes!

At last, with whistling scream, it strikes.

Cutting through the chancel-roof like paper,

The bomb

Explodes before the tabernacle of our dreams!

Rose-window warns with heightened hues

That buildings burn below the hill;

The town's on fire!

Up crescendo air-raid sirens' eerie call:

Take cover! — Where, in here?

Why would I go from you, Great Restfulness?

Where else?

Together let us stand while yet we may.

They'll not hunt me here — and if they do,

   They may only find my bones among your

                        rubble.

  I saw poor Coventry in ruins crushed

To staccato of machine-gun stutter

And snapping bark of anti-aircraft guns.

I saw the incendiaries flash,

The bombs like rain!

  Not here! Oh, halt them, God!

I heard torpedoes scream and crash;

Saw volcanoes of poor brick-work smashed,

Spewed up — as water by a stone is splashed —

The shattering of glass, out-burst.

  Invaders, may your savage seed be curst

For mothers' wails

Crying in extremity to God

Over children's bodies broken, rent

And bleeding on the dusty asphalt!

   God's Country!

   Planes! — Planes over playgrounds,

Over prayers for the dead — the freshly dead!

Useless! . . . . Uselessness!

   That hand, that baby hand — *a left!*

   Why not, foul vultures of the night,

Carry back this carrion,

These spilled-out entrails,

These poor severed hands

Back to those enslaved and trampled lands —

Go! —

And feed them to your vermined fledgelings

   Now nested in poor Flanders' fields of woe!

   This moisture on my palms!

Is it blood? . . . . or sweat of fear . . . . or tears?

Lachrymae Christi! . . . . Tears!

That's what he said:

With blood and sweat and tears.

Oh, steady! . . . . The dark — Golgotha's

Dark! —

Steadiness we need.

Steady me, dear walls of stone.

Where are you, walls? — The dark!

My sight — my day is gone.

Let my questing fingers touch you once again,

Even if I made this Darkness, too, myself —

This second coming of Golgotha. . . . .

The bombs are raining and the roof is rent. . . . .

Ah, walls, you're here, still cold and calm.

My heart's blood thunders in my ears.

But you are here. . . . .

And wood — and steel? . . . . A latch!

My little door, half-open, still ajar!

The Storm is brooding on your lintel yet.

But do not close — stand still ajar.

Mankind has mind-plague, door.

The world's wild winds

May never blow you shut.

You must remain for Man

His ultimate escape

From this returning curse,

His malady of mind.

For if at Armistice he sinks

Again to Apathy,

His eyes may never open on a better day;

And he,

Finding no Ararat of rescue,

In invited Deluge of obliteration

Must irretrievably be swept away.

These sturdy walls can stand some battering.

But twenty times their buttressed strength

Could not protect the hallowed Past

Beneath this roof so weak.

   For now the droning squadrons

Gather, teem and swarm

Across the choked vibrating sky.

The quickening flashes show the stone-dust

Hung upon the deathly air,

Hung and writhing like poor ghosts disturbed

By din of desecration —

Ghosts who, horror-muted, group and stare

Across the toppled candlesticks

Prone before that ragged gaping hole

We called an altar.

   Stone-dust

Raised by transient and destroying Science

Supplants the incense

   Of healing and repairing Time.

Ah, conquering slain!

Dear listening Dead,

Withhold all bitter and deserved disdain

At our poor boastful words:

'The War to end wars'. . . .

War again!

Triumphant slain!

You hear this querulous thunder

Of our feeble madness once again.

But despair not

Of our hope for betterment or cure.

Come, from your graves of sacrifice arise!

And with your dead but more enlightened eyes

Direct us to the Peace that must endure.

Be patient at your vigil, waiting dead.

Remembering the lessons of the Past, we now

Will pledge to you the sacred vow:

This time

Not only in our hearts

But through our hands and in our deeds

You will remain

And still live on — you *shall* live on,

   Victorious Slain!

www.ingramcontent.com/pod-product-compliance
Lightning Source LLC
Chambersburg PA
CBHW030731150426
42813CB00051B/409